# SO GLAD I'M ME

**Roddy Lumsden**'s first book *Yeah Yeah Yeah* (1997) was shortlisted for Forward and Saltire prizes. His second collection, *The Book of Love* (2000), a Poetry Book Society Choice, was shortlisted for the T.S. Eliot Prize. *Mischief Night: New & Selected Poems* (Bloodaxe Books, 2004) was a Poetry Book Society Recommendation. His later collections are *Third Wish Wasted* (2009), *Terrific Melancholy* (2011), *Not All Honey* (2014), which was shortlisted for the Saltire Society's Scottish Poetry Book of the Year Award, and *So Glad I'm Me* (2017). His anthology *Identity Parade: New British and Irish Poets* was published by Bloodaxe Books in 2010.

He is a freelance writer, specialising in quizzes and word puzzles, and has represented Scotland twice on BBC Radio 4's *Round Britain Quiz*. He has held several residencies, including ones with the City of Aberdeen, St Andrews Bay Hotel, and as "poet-in-residence" to the music industry when he co-wrote *The Message*, a book on poetry and pop music (Poetry Society, 1999). His other books include *Vitamin Q: a temple of trivia, lists and curious words* (Chambers Harrap, 2004). Born in St Andrews, he lived in Edinburgh for many years before moving to London.

RODDY LUMSDEN

# So Glad I'm Me

BLOODAXE BOOKS

ISBN: 978 1 78037 370 6

First published 2017 by
Bloodaxe Books Ltd,
Eastburn,
South Park,
Hexham,
Northumberland NE46 1BS.

**www.bloodaxebooks.com**
For further information about Bloodaxe titles
please visit our website or write to
the above address for a catalogue.

Supported using public funding by
ARTS COUNCIL
ENGLAND



Cover design: Neil Astley & Pamela Robertson-Pearce.

Printed in Great Britain by Bell & Bain Limited, Glasgow, Scotland, on
acid-free paper sourced from mills with FSC chain of custody certification.

## ACKNOWLEDGEMENTS

Acknowledgements are due to the editors of the following publications and websites where some of these poems first appeared: *Blue of Noon*, *New Boots and Pantisocracies* (Smokestack Books, 2016), *Poetry London*, *Poetry Wales* and *Prac Crit*.

Thanks to everyone who helped with the book.

# CONTENTS

TILL IT RUNS CLEAR

12 Simone's Cookie
13 Whitechapel
14 Equus
15 Brandade de Morue
16 Against Fucking
17 Rescuing Schrödinger's Cat
18 Autism
20 With a Cold Snap Clutching
21 So Glad I'm Me
22 Passing Pond Road
23 Kissing Edwin Morgan
24 Halfway Through the Year of the Horse
25 Bliss
27 Sehelleyan Orphan Trio
27 *Helleborine*
27 *Century Flower*
28 *Humroot*
28 Lily of the Valley
29 Union Mild Etch
31 Caliban Upon Settee / Dawn at Nikita's
32 Nikita's Wedding Dress
33 Our Children
34 Roddy Lumsden
36 Simone's Carouself

A SOFT LEVIATHAN

38 Jim Steinman / Jonesy
39 Coldplay / Foreplay
40 Willie Dixon / Safe
42 'F Troop' / Brotherhood
43 'Romeo and Juliet Are Drowning' / Beware Greeks
44 Back-up Flats

WITH ALL OF YOUR MIGHT


46 'The Night Has a Thousand Eyes' / Wader Swarm
47 Agnetha Fältskog in 1976 / Butterscotch
49 'Straight to Hell' / 'Thou art inclin'd to sleep'
50 A Band With Only Ten Good Songs
52 'I Wanna Testify' / Michael Donaghy
53 On the Death of Cilla Black
54 June Tabor Moving Room to Room
55 Alan Vega Brooding, Hotel Chelsea
56 Buying Shoes for Alex Chilton
57 Elvis Presley
58 In Bath with Madonna
59 Ghost Giraffes / Nico
60 Robin Holcomb Writes 'Like I Care'
61 'What Difference Does It Make?' / Maybe
62 'Even If My Mind Can't Tell You' / Jupitus Wakes
63 Remember To Kick It Over
65 Rock Chicks / Double Decker
66 So Much Synth (Mix Tape, Slight Return)
68 'Tender Object' / Cats on Windowsill


KIPPERS AND GLITTER


71 The Hoopoe
72 Bella #16
73 Bella #19
74 The Perfect Kiss
75 Musette / Cilice
76 Simple Dish / Speedboat
77 Caramac / Grand Romance
78 Hate
79 Work Crush
80 Baby's Cute and Mummy Too
81 False Flags / Khaki
83 Elba
84 My Kleos
85 May '15 EP
85 *Through Vicarage Avenue*
86 *Cameron*
87 *At The Standard*

88 Hoverfly
89 Halfway Through the Year of the Goat
90 Twenty-four Hours of People Saying Nope
92 Time Loop / Wishing Wells
93 Small Calamities
94 Jean Tester / Lionesses
95 Tending to the Reliable
97 Ashna Sarkar, Aged 5
98 Halfway Through the Year of the Monkey
100 The End of Fanny

# TILL IT RUNS CLEAR

## Simone's Cookie

So she eats it and wonders why it's gone.
Our predictive providers have divided
such an ontology. A well-knotted rope
of such thought is strung across the span.

She eats it. Groucho fiddles with a gag.
Kierkegaard delves its inner workings.
Is there cookie or is cookie a meltdown?
The step is a place for chewing on stuff.

Stuff. Such priss to call it that, when it
is everything. I'm thinking about everything.
Let me. I have erred toward the *disparu*
and have returned, buzzed, mildly majestic.

Half of that everything which I have lost
is lost to recapture. Here is the business:
you sit the step and you see down cookie
but logic pokes its fingers in your ribs.

It blows you, as a soap bubble is blown;
you remember awfulness, a sad station
you once waited on, or the acre of chaos
which pretends to be our understanding.

So often I have been halfway through cookie
and have not seen the punchline winging in.
Do we offer the object identity, or (a mind
swings slow open) ask its perfect answer?

The knots are too sturdy. The summer's warm.
Other stuff takes the mind. A book. A bird.
Parmenides sweated but loved the sun. Girl,
you ate the cookie and also are the cookie.

## Whitechapel

You lucked onto this side street,
a short strip where no one ever died.

All the children bicker round the shelter,
being hidden, edged or wide-eyed.

A paintable drayhorse runs throughout
your thought of being 'this will be a thought'.

Best sense itself? It is the first of all
our keen, known senses to disappear.

You turn the taps, force the pump, work
the locks of our tainted past, till it runs clear.

## Equus

Your eyes adjust to the cave murk at Lascaux.
Your fingers point to a breezy, marshed Camargue.
You dream of the gates of the Spanish Riding School.
Cob country pulses grassy in your arteries.

Statice and windflower thrive on the trodden machair.
You daydream of box saddles and training ropes.
You are Genghis bloodletting his beloved steed.
Patiently, Nina, you teach Clever Hans to count.

Bucephalus and Marengo nod in side-by-side stalls.
Your nightmare is a broken fence, the gone-dry trough.
You wash the malt-sweet scent of hay from dusty hair.
A straining chalk horse canters across your thought.

Your clifftop trek veers in the The Valley of the Rocks.
You stamp to Appleby tingling and breathless.
Four sets of jodhpurs sway on the line all night.
Some call this passion, but passion sinks beneath it.

## Brandade de Morue

*(i.m. Paul Reekie)*

If and when I venture to Zedel's, I will order
coquilles St Jacques in bubbling scallop shells
the like of which I plucked from the shore
at Balmerino. *Unspeakably toothsome*, you said
as we entered the Café Royal, hidden gems.
Parnassian sweetheart, prize arse who'd headbutt
a window mad for sweetest chorizo on display.
Pilot of a plane not yet invented, mutineer
on a bathtub boat sailing in all wrong directions.
Your telescope fixed on some cuckoo star.
Nimble spraffer. Nownik. Surely partly cat.
A host in one corpus. You had more edges
than Noel Coward who was far from the dare
of airflaps and buggy shades. 'I was at Paul's
last night' was shorthand enough to elicit
empathy. Once you played me Ornette Coleman
and I fled, seasick, to your bathtub's lip,
though woke next day to Ribena and codeine,
in the town where later you would slip that rope
around your bonny neck. Hell, Paul, come down,
I will cuddyback you up the long streak, jilt you
at the Barony, and the East End is ours: cooking,
smarts, spliff, blistery talk. The language is ours
to save. Most of our cohorts are drinking prose.
You were a fast one, absolutely. A helmsman
turned by their gutless rudder. Now the scallops
have gone cold. I'm lifting my pichet of Cahors
towards your sudden nothingness, which indeed
is allness, some scraped fact I will never reach.

## Against Fucking

So let's start here: I like it well enough,
there is conscience in it, for it sorts a night.
It has fed me many times. But it is never
at the deep of my go-aheading. The Mercator
of raunch needs to adjust his trusted map.
There are three sorts in this picture: the first
who tends to fetish, one who ruts and needs,
and another who warms to hands and mouths.
I'm not dim. I know crossover crosses over.
But I can point myself out in that picture.
And I'm not the caveman and I know my genes
need not fulfil my sense of failure, that sex
is no extreme sport, involving cannons, wire,
emotional exodus. And I need no costume,
just the quiet and the talk and touch of this.
We are moving against each other, thoughtwise
I mean, don't edge away. A night can last
without drowning to sleep, a sorry yard apart
with awkward looks. I like it well enough.
Yet *with* beats *on* or *in*. The trusted path
from swivelled eye to swyve is dusted now.
Hands and mouths are best. I fear you'll throw
those sideways. All is good but some is sweeter.
This palette has its many colours, this poem
its way too many metaphors, sorry, who
can sort this? Two cathartics going for it,
outdoing the tumble drier and those sirens?
I am not lazy, just prefer a pasture, or a boat
which moves slow, to some razed field of fucking.
The talking, the approach to need. I'd kiss.
But then we need to add the warm. I'd kiss.
But I want love how I want and I will look.

## Rescuing Schrödinger's Cat

Because I need him off the paradox
and onto my lap. There are Cheesies,
the night, and the lonely that he sorts.
I have majored in petting around jaw
and ear. The quantum has bored me
for some time now. The law is yum
and calm, not diddy flasks of poison.
Stop itching over what we cannot fix.
I am now simultaneously mostly okay
and mostly okay. The cat forgets the box,
the tuna helped. The Emmental strips
I set down on my knee. Now the only
superposition is this. The only season
summer, which draws him to a window.
Some brash people suggest I overthink.
Reality collapses? Oh sure, I know
the physicist is right. An apple head
is blinking; tail up, you are alive, Jim lad.
The bottle-goggled Austrian, bless his socks,
no way with women, is long gone dead.

# Autism

Some nights I catch the smell
                    of the lives of others,
all that is awry, agley,
                    the washers loose,
the springs rust-bunged.
                    Or the sheerest glee
I hope and fear that friends may feel:
                    their refound wallet
or the cat returned after a week
                    and just a little thin.
And when I say I smell this, I am
                    talking creosote,
broth smog, thinners. The room hangs
                    round the smell,
would bow to its bidding or bawl
                    at its funeral.
I strain to enter the life of another,
                    to bathe them, taunt them,
treat. For people mainly think they only
                    think they think that
no one thinks like them. But I too
                    have met against
your tarriest thought, your sick ambition,
                    lay late with a knife
in my mind, or a pulse of appalling glory.
                    We are alike as mercury
and nickel are, as leopard and gazelle
                    might blink in unison.
Even my siblings are disarmingly other.
                    And as a man walking
through all hours of darkness, clearing
                    to clearing, stile to well
to glebe to turnpike, I catch a gamey taint
                    of other beings, softly

being, grinding in foliage, cowering in boles,
zedding to warrens.
Paralleling you in bed, I give marginally less
of myself when sleep
grips its pliers. No one has ever known me.
Is that cute? I hear a woman
say, 'I died that night.' A man in the audience
shouts out in the quiet part
of the play. Some self-styled prophet screams,
full minute, on the beach
and all the poppets scatter from the sea,
gapey-eyed and clinging
at Mummy. I count these sifting colours
of my brief spectrum,
halfwise touching each in turn. You should
believe me when I say
that what I am seeing now is something
you must never see.

## With a Cold Snap Clutching

Thomas, did you ever turn your collar high
against the wind? Georgia O'Keeffe, who
sputtered steady southward, but one night
in a thin coat turned it up. Hello Delmore.
Plotting an essay, January in Brooklyn.
Meditating on it, though birding sprites
run through me and suggest your thoughts
were gruffer. You turned your collar up.
But this is London, giddy London, the city
the apple thinks it understands. Folklore
in every alley. Many of us are five hundred
and have never stopped to die, or heard
of the ontological quag that might arise,
night-brought. Death, yes, is for the other.
It is crisp though. Snowmen throw snowballs
all along my street and dream of eskimo pie.
To cool them, some chumps wrap their bones
round lampposts, their frost-buggered tongues
glued to the zero degrees of concrete poles.
I turn my noble collar up. It's just some shitty
green jerkin that I bought sometime, somewhere
but I am Cohen writing 'Dress Rehearsal Rag',
Pepys in a huff. Woolf collecting stones. Ouch,
not that one. The bitter blast avoids my scrag.
Milquetoasts, pantywaists, waifs and spies
of lesser pedigree, wimps, turn up that collar.
The night is not against us, just will not belong.

## So Glad I'm Me

Clare is waning: Warhol cameo girl * Sandy Denny, post-recording * tired girl with a coffee in a Fellini * sleepy writer after novel's end * Esther Greenwood roping in her thoughts * little sister on a bad night out * Antigone winding down * unsure system * zoo creature you have to learn and read the explanation of * daughter in a kitchen sink drama * stabled filly turning at the sight of snow * 'so glad I'm me' you wake to say * gold panned in a faraway stream * smoke * The Lady of the Fountain in the Mabinogion * oh, sleep, if sleep exists * Ponette grown up * Tinkerbell now glued to the idea of slinking home to the duvet * gypsy girl from the Flake advert * frustrated aviatrix * Lorna Doone escaping * all the lucky tousle is upon you * nodding, seeming downed by lady petrol * slump girl * tragedienne * Cohen's Nancy looking at the *Late Late Show* * Bedhead * this night is ending sweet * Jane Eyre with an eyepatch * Shakespeare, step in

## Passing Pond Road

The demons gave us symmetry, ducks synching
on the Princess pond, couple with prammed twins,
yoghurt which pretends but is a gluey composure
of diabolic symmetry. Swing door mood. Gumdrop face
of the bus stop schoolie. Hand. Hand. Mirror
cousining. The cactus rebels, arching to wherever
but at its succulent heart is balance; it ends up
a trier and failer at its, our, essential doubletude.
I button my coat and even the wind is on terms
with this, at my both sides. Parallax and syzygy
are second and third in this sapping league,
lapped by the monster of matching. Libra is its sign,
the bidden scales settling so; near stasis, your gaze
is now given to else: your own dear face, eye, eye,
nostril, nostril, the capital way that you are not
toppling. Symmetry will help you reach tomorrow.
And its twin tomorrow. Look – the pond is halved
by the bitty island. It shares its geese and terns.
Duality is management, necessity. We climb
to each other, aching a little, then, rocked to rest,
yearning so blithely to be that impossible – one.

## Kissing Edwin Morgan

seems uncanny because he is gay
and I am straight and because the day
is especially cold. A hungry kisser,
kissing him brings out the hive
that is him. A hive, are you with me?
Grey buildings. Check. Difficulties?
Check. I'm wrong for him, loose boy.
We are on a corner, of course we are,
then in an alley smooching. He talks
of the desert, distant rivers, Greekery,
the absolutes I will always fail to claim.
I smooth him. Rats run the terrace
we are dallying on. He nods, says yes.
To whatever. I hug him. Of course I do.
Love limits us, over, over, specialising
in this twisted limb of science. A bus
passes and we both wave to the world,
its merry passengers, its dour chance.
I have a train or plane to catch, I pat
his perfect shoulder, say farewell.
And then it is the night, alone. Night,
the second best escape; walk, walk in
a heavy coat. Maybe the future needs you.

# Halfway Through the Year of the Horse

Village. Walking down with Rosie and Jennybear
and The Crusader and we are not saying much.
Since we do not have to; the best of friendship
evolves to silence. Trouble has ridden the backs
of each of us, recent times. Evenings swab away
in the very centre of silence. Evenings at Amy's
when Bambam and Minnie May don't miaow,
evenings when Nina high fills the water trough
in the stews of silence between the whinnying
of Pep and Graylie. The negative need not
be negative. Listen now, there is nothing
but the creak and breath which prove silence.
A sudden mouse tries silence then enhances it.
A sudden horse, sound turned down, cruises
the bend to the last. Sleep is the least of silence.
Bustle, gabbing, can crush, chainsaw, go find
your corners. Jennybear is texting. Rosie paints
her nails in a room where only herself persists.
Silent update request, silent train, just too far
to hear. Salt, pepper, and often the heart stick
to the muted dominions we gather elsewhere
than the head, that brawling champion of noise.
Is silence fear? Desire? Cousin to both poles.
Preference arises from the baseline of silence,
coordinates of murmur or yowl. Now you stand
all hushed, computing this sandwich's filling.
What should be in and what must be silenced?
Back-up, coast, entertain a pittance of leeway.
Let up. Go to the rug, since much silence is low
in a room. Slow in a room. A mouth gone closed.
Emperors, you did not favour it. You clambered
and rode the horse and whipped it to snorting
when it wanted the meadow, the sugared grass,
the tale of there not being a tale, some nothing.

## Bliss

*(for MJS)*

I

* The seismologist counts the stout trees down an avenue. * Still there. * An octopus kicks across sand at depth, its best of hormones clanking. * Unsudden laughter at the coven and pussycats leaping. * Swans in transcendent flight. * The faerie people sink drunk on fiddle tunes. * The sea cook jumps off starboard to the onshore. * Most charming of all chimeras seeding your dream. * Beetle sunning itself. * The in-crowd smoke hard in the basement, the night to come. * A cinematic pulse which throbs some evenings. * The prestidigitator's flourish. * A kiwi's bob. * The sherbet of liaison. * An opening chord which sighs us. * Bliss. * Laser rays mating. * Swooning protons. * Chaos grinning at its business. * The oceans in our heads. * The jogtrot pace of the better of our days. *

II

* The weasel settles snug in her nest of twigs. * Our twosome walks, too few. * A semi-precious stone rolled in a hand in a daydream in a valley. * Segue of thought. * Then finding your tribes. * Vaccine against all shine-lack climbs our blood. * Now the scribe sets down the perfect sigma, the pristine theta. * Palomino mane shaking. * Park bench conversation. * Hood up in snowy wood. * Break the tape, cut the cake, snip the ribbon. * Cat purrs on lap, 4am. * A lean against a red brick wall. * Too few. * Pad Thai. * I roll down the slope and you behind me, laughing. * The bichon frise gives you a paw. * Cream. * A good game of snap. * The good-hearted stranger smiling. * A thriving meadow where celandines nod toward where we may have lain talking, sorting all of our imperfections. *

III

Splash. * This cathedral defies our *par delictum.* * I feel I have the suitable ten up my sleeve. * Warm air on skin. * Hope coming to surface. * Comfort, that winmost beast. * A lie-in. * High score. * To seem the self and like it. * Conches rolling in the tide-swill. * A gathering, a jam, a picnic. * Corner kissing. * Scritching a breathy black Lab. * Road to the holiday. * Red lollipops. * I could be happy. * Best air of all the airs. * The masseuse pats and tempers me, lively with the day. * Tequila. * And you are smiling now. * The candle does what a candle does and neatly. * When I dance, I dance alone, like this. * Kicking the tragedy. * Paths which bless us. * The camel tumbles dopey on its unsunned side. * Our sing-song faces. * All cantering entities. * Mornings when I believe in bliss and give up, give in. *

## Sehelleyan Orphan Trio

*(i.m. Caroline Crawley)*

### *Helleborine*

My little brother, my little other,
dull at the ribs and drooping.
Six in the morning says you;
by seven we are talking otherness.

The pillar box, the roar on the sea.
We have else to talk over. Sorry.
Widespread and scattered too.
That's an act. I grew only once.

Never a virgin and never a tramp,
snaking to sky. Hero boy. Bloom
who burst then took your time.
I would have you on my team.

Thirty inches of grump, just not
the family's prizest of candidates.
I would share a bedroom with you,
read to you even when you sleep.

### *Century Flower*

Notice the pard, true to his task,
sniffing the pale grass for traces;

the brock upchucking soil in some
backwater coppice, avid for peanuts;

the helminth, now easing through
its underworld of tilth or gut,

none of our business. And the Queen
of the Andes, brazen in its centennial

fruition, a sunburst torch, shaming
or blaming the earth with glory.

## *Humroot*

What are you, creeping soma, studding up
through sand or soil? My little bell, cowslip

in which Ariel slumped in his misty sleep.
A buzzing worm below my thought, a snowdrop

sent to naughty step. Toddler climbed to shedtop
and swearing to jump. Perhaps a rusty cup

a widow sets her nose to, country walk. A sip
of meadow air. On form, gistless, non-stop,

bonnie thought, bitter thought, you crawler, shop-
bought bloom, or tendrilling, rainforest trap

for incy wincies. Or pushing through clover, all hope.
I like the think of you. Root, root. Rise and slap

my silliness. Turn me off. Spin off this humming tap
of fancy speculation. Grow, will you? Nope then yep.

## Lily of the Valley

I carry the purse of memoir, just here where
conval lily arcs and points the wood edge,
its farnesol luring the courting nightingale.

It treats my heart and peps my buzzed memory.
Its cooling gladiates of leaf, its dapper string
of closedmouth bells. All that I'll recall.

Pestle it; its juice recruits my thinking.
I swoon against a beech tree, the only movement
these swaying blooms and glory coming back to me.

## Union Mild Etch

> 'a newly recognised disorder, on almond scions
> growing on Marianna 2624 Rootstock'

I do not know myself. Is that familiar?
I walk down, but walk down selfless

some days. I have named the holes
on a golf course; I have walked wrong,

listened to 'Danelectro 2' feeling it was
part of me. I have rarely lied, for lying

leads to tigerish impassion. Almonds
are not my thing. I had a student once

who used to bring them in. To unknow
what and who you are is frankly, thanks,

a bit of a scare. My scions are none.
I long to give my gift to the big night,

but the night turns on me and gasps an ouch.
Who are you? says someone, but I'm no one.

## Caliban Upon Settee / Dawn at Nikita's

Ah spirits! We may as well finish this vodka,
says Ariel, topping my glass. We are listening
to 'Leaders of Men', then 'The WASP' then
'Ten Storey Love Song', then 'Leaders of Men',
one more time. Light thinks to leak. Impartial.
'I've got the spirit but lose the feeling'. Meaning
I lose the will to stand and resort to my animal
four-footedness, salvage to the happy situation.
Crawling for frogs, crawling for my purpose,
but in my proudness admitting that the spirits
have knocked me. Thank you bold Stephano.
For brewing my unbalance. My bolthole
is three minutes hence, but Ariel knows
she must throw over me the gaberdine, yes,
a duvet in reality and reposition me, crash
herself and sleep will come. Yet the sofa
welcomes me. I am standing in my way.
When we sleep in our clothes, we retain
our character. Caliban, I whisper, remember
this world is ours. But all the new people
tempt us to spirits. We wake late, of course,
and Ariel makes tea, fresher than the groaner,
aging beast. She slips on Otis Blue. The change
that is gonna come is a change of clothes.
Luck and magic mean I know to wear them.
Hair of the dog, says Caliban. Hair of the pizza,
says Ariel, Tupac and Curtis still smoking
on her wall, job done, as all bad jobs need doing.
There is dying young and there is dying like this.

## Nikita's Wedding Dress

All this gossip and me saying we will be married
by the year's end. And you saying, no, by spring.
And the pollen is already singing; maybe, lady,
I ought to shop for a suit. But this is joshing:
who could waltz to 'Candidate'? Or foxtrot
to 'New Dawn Fades'? Besides, it is not that.
First dance? No, a thing more simple will do.
I'll teach you, a different dance. Curtis glooms
on your bedroom wall. We will and can friend up.
Allow me this though: that your dress would be
the best of black, of course, sitting all over you.
Black satin, black lace and black girl within.
Unknown pleasures. But we need not, will not
marry. Pushed to no limit. The dress is lovely
but will widen the eyes of some drawn one
neither of us know. May it happen. I'll teach you
and you will marry in black, walk smile-charmed
to your hotel while others are still at their dancing.

## Our Children

Shanikwa, we have given you
your traditional Scottish name
since your nine-times-great grandfather
was likely named Shanikwa, as he
sneaked across the glens, hoping
to spear a Jacobite cad, longing
to split the soft, white belly
of a mountain hare, to sing out
the praises of its death, in the tongue
of the Gaels, last light shaking the gorse.

Morag, we have given you
your traditional Zambian name
which means 'strong mare' or 'leader
of an all woman army'. Your auntie
was a Morag, as were all your aunties.
Your forebears were tattooed with horses,
war arrows and the name Morag, blue
on brown. One day, you will lead
the great rebellion which, as yet,
does not bear the noble name we chose.

But did not choose, for names choose us.
The systems of our socialist republics
bow to our patro- / matronymics, bow
to our praise names – your mother Nikita
named after a Bolshevik warrioress;
me named after a mad Prussian prince
who spent mornings shooting rats, plotting
against the ruling class. Our children,
we have placed upon you the best names
that we know. Now outdo us. Outlive us.

## Roddy Lumsden

To John Graham Mellor, in the hope he is still alive.
Not all lives are buns and not all buns are frosted.
Times there are two of us, umpteen of us, caging
that we are not the doppelganger, which the real?
Stuart Goddard. Self-exported imitations. Vain
coincidences. The real as freakish. The double
as shrug or wide eye – you're me too? Oh, hell.
Who were you? Oh, I was all too busy being me.
I refused to be me, though some sweetheart
wrote it once, bored in an exam, and ringed it
with a biro heart. Someone spilled the gossip.
The wind ploughed on. Roberta Joan Anderson.
How many Jane Smiths walk the boroughs,
clicking the eyes of Paul Joneses. Afterwards,
it may matter less. James Newell Osterberg Jr.
You take the name as if you take a punishment.
Most are wrong named and they sense the treat
they might have been. They try on the tilted hats
of names, Romulus, Roscoe, Magenta Ruthie.
Some cross the line, the only name in the race:
Mungo Penfold I recall, or Gilford Mentiply,
my second cousin. Hello Martha Sprackland.
Attorney N'chunga N'chunga who sent me poems.
Collect your sash. The double will not seek you
or friend you or grim when they self-Google.
Eleanora Fagan Gough. Steady, Roddy, I am
getting round to you. Do you want this yum yum?
Name is not policy. It's rumour been superglued.
I've heard of you, a stranger says. Another flicks
the directory and figures, number blocked. Y name,
Z name, name numbed to extinction by sick history.
A phone rings and we all answer it. Yes, I am he.
I am not he. Wrong number. Władziu Lee Valentino.
Roddy Lumsden, maybe watching *Breaking Bad*,

box set, in Alexandria, you, my only namesake,
we should never meet. How dare you, we would say,
the quirk of our link gone quick. I couldn't like you.
Christine Anne Perfect. I telephone my mother,
Mrs Lumsden, née Miss Lumsden. My one demand
is my real name. But she is not taking this call.

## Simone's Carouself

A little battle. As in right now when I want
to pull a cover over someone sick, mop up,
call someone relevant. To make all better.

Then shirk the us. Us being the downtime
of the self. I need alone. Alone is whittling,
here where some auteur might mistake me.

The insofar. A turning stable. The mount
is linguine maned, shiny to the nimbled hoof,
and oh you go with loop, unable to alone.

Identity is the flimsiest of damned systems
yet I am holding its pole, going pony round.
Giddy, but at times hoping to be recognised.

Eleatic, but stuttered. I do know who I am;
each twirl hints at the brink of a becoming.
A filmmaker casts me, some photographer

dips me in his contagious notion of ink
and somehow that's me. No, but thank you.
I'll self it. Determined, avoiding my other.

The spinny edge is daring but look within.
Simone, we are centred but centres are things
we can't wager with, lass. Now and not ever.

# A SOFT LEVIATHAN

I look like a woman on the run!

RAINA PARRIS

## Jim Steinman / Jonesy

Amber Eyes is running the room, a child on fire.
It's the climby part of 'For Crying Out Loud'
that is doing it for her. It is just Lloyd Webber
with attitude, I tell her. She's not much pleased.
The ginger tom named from *Aliens* is tongue deep
in kitten milk. The fruity sack at his netherhood
won't be there at month's end. And if I worry on
all melodrama, would you blame my silly guess?
Your love is like a shadow on me all of the time.
Meat Loaf stepped out of Marvel, heaving, much
as Marvin Lee Aday stepped sweaty to the shower.
Her step-aunt photos us. We are Sonny and Cher.
Only the drinks have made us cross-photogenic.
She is Cher at nineteen. I am Sonny, two months
after his skis hit the tree. In LA, Steinman snacks,
late, on decaf, a cinnamon muffin and FM radio.
He has spent the evening sketching Tchaikovsky.
Alas, the bat is not yet out of our hell. It is late
and rare is the occasion when four in the morning
is not some scene from a movie as yet unmade
and for the proper reasons. Jonesy, chase this.
Amber Eyes, maybe turn that down just a little?
Tchaikovsky sweated the details of *The Nutcracker*.
Jonesy sleeps in a box lined with a Jigsaw sweater.
My gran, not a drinker, looked drunk in all photos.
Shall I hold you tight? We woke the neighbours.
But we chose rock and roll and days come when
the only available work is waking the neighbours.

## Coldplay / Foreplay

Amber Eyes has pulled her top up to her neck
and her hands are down her barely-there shorts.
She's on the floor. She is blaring out 'Clocks'.
It's late. Her ginger kitten bounces, bemused.
I'm on the couch, a boat which I have sailed
on previous voyages. She is Martha and Mary,
by which I mean Graham and Millington,
busy in her interpretive raunch. Her wine done.
Is this to turn me on? But there is also night,
rehearsed by the tall and tree-dimmed window.
So, kitten, night, cider, cigarettes and sofa
and masturbating girl. I sense there is worse.
In a minute, I will jump ship and join her,
and you can guess where my hands will go,
which way I'll swim. The carpet's woozy waves.
The twists and shifts and games of eyes and mouths
before bed swallows us. A soft leviathan.

## Willie Dixon / Safe

Amber Eyes is speaking, not for the first time,
about prevailing good. We need meat, she says
and, she on lamb, me on spatchcock, she asks
'How do we know we are safe?' then, 'Why
are you an atheist?' I talk of cogency, how
proof is not my agency. I spit an olive pit,
think of the bitter men and limited women
who taught me Bible. Blues. Safer, safest.
The chalice I do not need, the colour purple,
the chasubles which stink with utmost foust
in kists. Oh lord. Those whose one yard stare
has redemption on its needle end. Desperate.
The moment did not happen when I entered
a dim shop and asked for chance and handed
a pound note for all-to-be-well. My anchor
is not in the rock, thank you, ladies and gents.
'Blues is the root and all music is bearing
the fruit.' Some believe this. Some believe.
Yes, I woke up this morning. It wasn't tough.
My mind did not mount a unicorn, set out
for Helicon. It reached for a NutRageous
and the alloy of awfuldom and felicity
that would make my day. America sat out
most of my ancestors' centuries, reinvented
all. I pull a flag out from the moon of my head.
And now I am Willie Dixon, may as well be,
reinvented, six foot six, river-deep, calling
for the whuffling harp and tinkle tankle
stand-up that might define my soul. I wrote
the song of songs and had it stolen, found it
in the mouths of safer others. So simple,
my recipe, but so few followed. Done wrong.
Done wrong. Heaven has no back door.
My life is free of rooster crow and wail.

I reach for self not science. I am not safe.
But crème brûlée might help, or Amber Eyes,
as she does, kissing my nape, unexpected,
as my mother did before I was enlightened,
before I thought I knew I knew all this.

## ‘F Troop’ / Brotherhood

Amber Eyes is sitting, sitting it out.
We have beer, a guitar and her brother
and the show will start. Sonsy boy,
better than me at the singing, but that
is what we will do. Duets. Cohen,
yes, mostly. *My brother, my killer.*
Blood climbs, but often only so far.
*Dancing round the jukebox with*
*my brother.* He has amber eyes too.
Good player. People think my friend
Tim and I are brothers. Well, we are.
But not. Hark to the accents, blood
we need not share; hope, yes, hope
and that apt charge of recognition.
My own brothers roost, different
birds, different beasts, but we are blood,
named and renamed, as siblings are.
Amber Eyes photographs her brother
and me singing ‘Famous Blue Raincoat’.
Not quite the Everlys. We sing, we talk
of Archie Roach, the outback singer,
stolen generation; let’s sing another;
*let’s get another.* We seek our haven.
The Champion Hotel. A decent corner.
We seek our brothers. Kindness leaks
into us. Kindness and kinhood seep
into us softly, I hope, much as we need.

## ‘Romeo and Juliet Are Drowning’ / Beware Greeks

Our sorrows perhaps. Amber Eyes has blonded,
soft for once. I don’t get called *those names.*
‘I would die for you’, her aunt said; the Greeks,
the Italians, what are they like? Not enough oats.
I have no gifts, just a cardigan and a decent manner.

You can ditch your purchases, baddest things
go easy into a simple ditch and sink. So rarely
have I prepared. Don’t come to me for espionage
or the bottom layers of treason. Who would build
a muckle horse, to take a city that will disappear?

The idea of the Greeks appeals to me: a hurdle
I have not been over. *Mad if you want her*
*and mad if you don’t.* I do, but the moving in
is edgy. *When my son moves out.* Romeo fears
that Juliet might drown. Troy swivels in maybeness.

The select force ready to break from the sculpted
cuddy. Will I move in? I may. ‘I would die for you.’
I would cook for you, Juliet. Walk to quiet places.
*Till the others arrive.* It is okay – aged, we understand
these: honey and danger, the just about tough.

## Back-up Flats

Amber Eyes is trying out her stilettos,
criss-crossing the seagrass rug. She
is brushing up for Beating Retreat,
the annual military ceremony in town.
Music? Anything but Snow Patrol,
I tell her and she plays a full hour
of Chopin. I cook her fricadelles,
spiced black eyed beans and cajun
fennel ketchup. There is a bible
on the table, an occasional creep-up
inch of scarlet knickers. Her son
and her ginger kitten re- and disappear
throughout the afternoon. She offers
a hooped cashmere top which belonged
to her dead ex. I am mildly feverish.
Sit, feet up here, she says and this
will cheer you: she puts on a sitcom.
Now, her goosey voice punctuates
the sun-spilled afternoon. She tousles,
irons, readies. My fancy lunch a bit part
in her day. Addled governess, no-go area,
maddest of lasses, marchioness of sorters,
she struts, oh bloody hell, then seeks
her back-up flats, slots them, as you do,
into a shoulder bag. After the drums
tattoo and paradiddle, after four glasses
of Sauvignon, after her ritual rolling
of eyes at whatever, she will still
look swish, but she will lose those shoes.

# WITH ALL OF YOUR MIGHT

## ‘The Night Has a Thousand Eyes’ / Wader Swarm

The knots burst, the rails break. You are seventeen
and this song plays in a shoddy café where coffee
is still a prototype. Not your thing and also not
your thing. Your feet tap, that skippy rhythm
demands it, though you press your new flats
to the tacky floor, taking care now not to be seen
to like it, which you do not. The boy from Fargo
swings his shoulders; he did not take to the air
on the day the music died. There are these songs
about clumsy phone calls: ‘He’ll Have To Go’,
‘Diamonds and Rust’, and this. Men and women.
Sometimes we’re hopeless. Women and women too.
And I’m calling you now. Oh. ‘Tough old bird,’
you called yourself, when I hugged you, and me
your little Lambeth pal, walking where we do not
want you to walk. You are dying. I wish we had
another word for it. In a booth in the Mid West,
Dylan is evermore spinning his nicotiney finger,
calling Baez. Reeves, all of us, may not hear
the words we want to hear. In Norfolk, waders
surge and lift. You are with love. The many wings.
And care and careful watch is all. What’s best. Just
a thousand eyes? For the day has twenty, and there
they swivel, close to task. In splendid plenitude.
They are as you are. Wanted. Swaggering. True.

## Agnetha Fältskog in 1976 / Butterscotch

All that we are not. We are walking down
and I am handing out butterscotch. Rosie
is unsure, Jennybear chucks hers. Scotched
or scorched, brown sugar dumbed to sugar free.
I finish mine, undo the boiling, stomachwards.
It's what Rosie said earlier: 'This is strange,'
when 'Dancing Queen' tripped forthwards
from before she existed, to the prompt moment.
And it is. All profitable art pivots in the dare
of our contention. What were we? What are?
Achieving. The soft crack stage and the boil
knocked back. 'Similar to toffee'. Mmm. Similar
to the ghost of The Beatles you can haul down
from the song. To the embryo of 'Oliver's Army'
you can stop and taste as if there was pre-taste.
Bushbaby. Lofn. Goldilocks. Champagne Aretha,
crowd eyes are on us now. We have history.
Europe buzzes under heat. You were a mother.
Sync slid and we could never have danced.
Those yellow labels. Tuppenies on the stylus.
Epic. I was a boy child who needed nothing
or so I say. The world came for you, coming
to the boil. The decade's caramel. Men still lie
against their wallflower walls. Weak for beauty
and dimmed by shame. I know. This is strange.
With butterscotch, it used to be more simple,
the poppet yumming, sticks slid from a pack,
a grandpa leaning; danger had the volume down
and the safe song reeled you. I might dance,
the perfect being something I might give in to,
not wriggling in sweat as the real slow spinned.
Nil choice but to be what I am now, roped
onto these top edge glyphs, convinced, yes,
that I am better. Double meaning. I get you.

Double meaning. All that we are not. I will
retire now, risking melody, beauty, simple.
The cat squeal at the song's first promise.
I'll lie. Planning my rude dance out of this:
alwaysness and breathing, bother and alibi.

## ‘Straight to Hell’ / ‘Thou art inclin’d to sleep’

Let me tell you about your blood, marmalade coat one,
quirky, eating Nik Naks, far from any island, except
that this is an island; coast prompts fear and we forget.
I sit half a carriage away or else I’d stare. A gentle man.

Doing right costs me my blood. Not a one-liner type.
Judge me please on my sympathies or better yet
do not judge me. Anaemia, a father ill. Right wronged
by right. Any frontier? The edge at which Miranda slept.

And brave new train. Sleigh bed in which now you sleep
so slinkingly unaware I saw you. So right all along
to strike the peace of me not knowing you. Allowed:
the blood of awkwardness or fraughtness. Allowed:

a head tilt and displacing thoughts of whatever else,
an iron racing, a sleepy chance to chance your pulse.

congregate. They meet on the Old Kent Road.
One of them is high, pretty much forever.
They talk about Vashti Bunyan and, a stretch,
Beck, how collaboration might be the future.
A mouse rounds their feet, since it must do,
this is Old Kent Road. They used to nail it.
But only ten nails went in. Now will they be
remembered by anyone but David, who loves
the B-sides and has blu-tacked the cover art
in his garage? The band has the girl singer
who is shall we say blooming. The drummer
is divorcing. The kit is cobwebby. They need
eleven to go to prom, to go to Pitchfork pick-up.
The new direction might be tinged with psych.
Why not? Or let's youtube 'Ride a White Swan'
and we'll see what that brings to the sad picnic
of progression. Richard is in theory in charge
but luck's not on him, just as prosecco is not
in their vases of Stella. What if we bring jazz
to the table? Subtle of course. Or drumming
in the style favoured in highlife? Two of them
slept in their clothes last night and are itchy.
Maybe they should move on to the Amersham?
Doug has a couple of possibilities for gigs.
Doug mentions the thread on BCB, one which
was mainly thumbs high. Only one or two pissers.
Vinyl is back, says the girl, her name remembered
less than her pout. They can work the third album.
Maybe if we vamp the volume or dress the same,
in yellow. An instrumental always lifts a record.
Someone, as ever, has a photographer friend,
another knows what some call a graphic designer.
Cello is in. Apparently. Nick Drake has an appeal
of sorts. McCartney and Richards wrote during sleep

so they will too, if the tossing stops and the lager
stops being the syrupy impetus to the mediocre.
Ferry crunching 'Virginia Plain', or Stevie Nicks
undoing Buckingham. Wah. They've ten good songs.
And the scratchy side of nowhere is right where
they are going – you got that. Richard has enough
for a cab to the Amersham. But he is several miles
from 'Will You Love Me Tomorrow'. A county away
from 'He'll Have to Go'. Lovers, I love you all.

## ‘I Wanna Testify’ / Michael Donaghy

I am in his kitchen with Donaghy and one of three things
might happen: a strong coffee, a large good vodka, or
he will ask me to testify. Instead he says this: ‘Next,
do something serious.’ The place is sweetly ramshackle.
I have recently lucked and scored his first slim volume
in a dive book place in San Francisco. The froth needs
to be skimmed from my coffee, by which I mean poetry.
It’s off Green Lanes, 2001, pale room, and Michael
a shade too young to be my uncle, but I’ve asked him.
Noises off. But for now it’s a rare two-hander with
the man whose wrangled work I will walk through
and walk through until. His fine hands are clasped.
I have my doubts about him, as is the best of practice.
Once, he sneaked and left a poem in my bedroom;
I’m never sure why. Once, he did everything, or said
he did, which is the best of practice. I’m thinking kebab
(it’s Green Lanes) or grabbing him to the pub. A hundred
rewrites of his latest poem he says. These days I trust
myself to one – more Gauguin than Russian novelist
with amanuensis sitting await. Yet there was no testis,
two won’t do and I’m not dropping down to my knees
for Donaghy, Christ or James Brown. Clinton wrote
the song on an envelope in a diner booth. Hello Michael.
You did not need to prove. Rust will rise. Haloes
will settle on the satin hair of saints. All those fellows
on the centre of a bridge are in more danger. Inquisitive
friends will be doggone. For I unbecame a Christian,
which was necessary. More coffee please and that joke
about the apple. And I will take your mantle of gossip
and wear it best, friend. And, yes, will get more serious.

## On the Death of Cilla Black

The whispering, system down, the unforeseen.
Bad turns. A sorry not accepted. An afternoon

which rotted to boredom. The cityscape in flight.
Surround yourself. To be should be what might.

I thought to sing but was not wanted. Fares
we have to pay since others do demand. They're

waved or waived. To be misunderstood
is modesty enacted. So she stood

and held. She took my coat, she winked and grinned
in sitting rooms which flicker in the mind.

She became, became, became. Love crawls
below us, does it not? Success unwheels

above, above, snowlike. Supposed random,
as she tilts from the someone to the seldom.

## June Tabor Moving Room to Room

To know what you know and what you can't
is half of it. The singer plans her stance.

Definition: to be. And be the bellwether
and not the nestlecock. She is in the other

room and is plumping a cushion. Intrigue
slides through a few unwashed dishes. Tig

is played in a shabby park an hour away.
We know this. All the stolen swag sways

in dusty garages. Rust grasps, our sour age
grinds. When I sing, I sing through courage

and all landscape disappears. Damned air
draws her and she throws back her hair.

Words come to her then because she moves.
Everything has something to do with love.

## Alan Vega Brooding, Hotel Chelsea

Not half reptile. The danger looking me up and down.
Don't call it twilight – it's not so pretty. I'm on one leg.
Hell already but the evening is ticking as it well might.
Shall we usher the night? The rope and chain say all.

Fire says yes, it always will. And there is an Irish bar
within a block will let us do anything, till any time.
I'll have what I always have: haywire and backchat.
I'm in this for debris, or the slowest of snowfalls.

I slide between random and the absolute, any good
man will, cautious to talk less slick than his logic.
To be among the cross street gods, you have to speak
or sing. Press by me softly now, for I am thoughtful.

## Buying Shoes for Alex Chilton

So he needs them and we head towards the centre
of whichever city. He is shaky and it is years
since he bought shoes. I have problems too,
buying shoes; not in my nature. And haircuts.
And he says yes, me too; I am touchy in his company.
I plan to die after him but to recall him at my end.
We're gonna get born. And Cuban heels are what
I fancy for the little man from Memphis. The lady
smells him, and I'm little better. Then he points,
as on the back cover of *Radio City* at bad skis,
at ropey footwear. Nico never looked twice at him.
But he wrote 'Stroke It Noel' and life is rich, rich.
Yet we have the issue with these shoes; his boots
are reeking, there are rumours of some espadrilles
in a cupboard where a goldfish swims, some song
sweet sung. Wedges, poor sir, platforms, we can do
something for you. Chilton, you need your shoes.
Stand outside and I will buy for you. This corner
is where you will try them, solemn. This and that
is the way you will try them, but they will fit.
I know the way. This is why I am with you. We're
gonna get born. Let's catch that last train, you
turning your feet one way and another, telling me,
bad choice, buddy, I do not know why I started
to talk to you. How the hell do I even know you?

## Elvis Presley

Science club has established a scale for the distance
between polka dots, for between the blackstick nests
of roosting rooks. A new desk diary and a woman sits
close to dusktime and red inks her predicted on dates.
For the lord's sake, we take bleak and callous tests
of dot to dot. Not quite Abraham, we sulk and next
day seek, skimming the digital downtowns of twoness,
their silky-windowed blocks, for what may tame us,
for the on/off skill of the king, that we might stand,
one schtick shoe in amnion, one schlock shoe in dust.

## In Bath with Madonna

We are awkward and listening to Rachel's,
the *Music for Egon Schiele* album. We fit,
just about. Of course, we play with soap
and eye each other. Now, her knotty ankle
dandles on my thigh. Much that she has done
has been discussed. I'm a bluebell thrumming
in its season, causing no rebellion. Our aim
is not to wash our hair, for this is intimate.
She has eight years on me, and two legs
which danced the world. So I suffer this.
More hot. Ciccone, we got nude, twisted
these taps. We both can gulp and see our us.
The issue is that I know your mistakes
and I am clever but simple. Pass the soap.
I see what you have and you can go for me
if that tickles. I wonder if you were ever real.
Then we rise from this solemn water, to towels,
to tumble, then, humming quietly, to the gentle.

# Ghost Giraffes / Nico

> Until about two years ago, I thought giraffes were made up,
> like ghosts.
>
> JENNY CONROY

Until about now, I forgot there were no giraffes in Nico.
Most or many things: candles, morphine, the primroses,
the crown prince and the reluctant princess who cameo
in different songs. Oddest thoughts require their phases.

Camelopard. Ungulate. Ruminant. Wraith, migrating
towards this or that browsed acacia and my estimate
is that none yet swum the Niger, with that vibrating
Teutonic buttered voice within, or with the obstinate

hour hand of all of this crawling, calculating the fuss.
The giraffe is part real, or more real than the unicorn.
It turns its neck and what it sees is Africa and us.
Nico glimpsed the avant garde and us and heroin.

The ghost giraffe, the real giraffe walk hoof in hoof.
They're real and not but also not and real. Decide.
A bestiary drops open. Warhol claims there is no truth.
Some of us said things but, yes, some of us lied.

## Robin Holcomb Writes 'Like I Care'

Was I in love then? A century gentling
off from its source. And falling already
on remedy. Or before a turn which matters
only to source. The quilt on a chairback.

The crooked door. The porch's tarry rope.
And tutting, self-tut. The singer's on-pull
towards happen. The justice of between.
The piano stubborn, a bull piqued by darts.

The piano's storm day wilt. Burnt skill.
A new hymn knocks an old one, much
as fresh love shakes a room. Its filching
on us, our dogdamnit travels through it.

Threads dry in best of sun. I was in love.
On that I bet a half of what I've gathered.

# ‘What Difference Does It Make?’ / Maybe

Ah, Summer ’84 and a lass who will become my first love,
Lady Rebecca, sits bonny as ever and we play The Smiths.
Mania is on me like baddest caramel. She’s fine with me.
We find each other don’t we? Words, hugs are the dot-to-dot
of all but idiots. We will go on. Me to some dark varsity
with somewhat significance, she to NYC, acting, dancing
until those hurt. The folksong of how we met is so long
and strange that I dropped it from my repertoire. Never
will I dance with anyone but the good one who taught me.

Still ill? Roads back are not to be travelled too often.
The future is a poor friend. Still is. Then a teddy bear
she found for me and, asking if I had a name for him,
I said ‘Maybe’, meaning maybe. Now still he reclines
in my childhood bedroom, the ghost of Morrissey
close clinging to him, brown and button-eyed, arms
open to all the possibilities that never came for me,
for us. I hugged him last Christmas, the sad child
that hunkers in us all rising to undrowned surface.

Back to the old house. Not as old as Lady Rebecca’s,
with its bestiary on the Great Hall ceiling, targes,
the four-poster where MQOS lay fretting, topiary,
a tennis court where she recited from *Lovers, Winners*,
Mag and Joc going down. That charming bogman
Morrissey lies turning; I aim to outlive that man.
All men have secrets and here is mine: I am capable
of the best of love and so few are. Maybe is in silence.
Some day I hope he gasps and coughs and comes to life.

## ‘Even If My Mind Can’t Tell You’ / Jupitus Wakes

‘My hopes, my dreams.’ First morning it is the licking
tongues of kittens, twitch, itch. All bonnie is uncanny.

Not dreaming, but waking thought. The scene stolen.
Second it is something none can put a taut name to.

Third is the angle of a blind, a dumb waste of thought
but it carries him on its shoulders till mid-afternoon.

Next, the unsteady gift of a mirror waiting for not him,
but us. That it will showboat, that it will steal our eyes.

Day five and it is spiders but he canters past all that.
There is a script. And our readthrough may well do,

or may well not. Six, and a swank yacht which flies
into thought. A swan behind it. ‘You fill the screen.’

Seven and seven is. Card swiped. You set the scene.
Stuff done, and you come to. And, aye, you know it.

## Remember to Kick It Over

When a new tide bothers the shoreline
and does for the fort we spent hot hours
spiffing, I see I am easy to the business
of giving over, which is not giving in.

Hello Rachael Allen, buy me a drink,
then nudge me sideways. I'm now ripe
to become Bowie in his Berlin years.
The lease is long up on my new kid.

And, okay, the bubblegum has gone
a little rubbery in my mouth. Youth
was something I never had anyway,
born as an adult of questionable sort.

We will move on from this car park
to the other one we were eyeing up.
Though we will watch you from there.
Distance is a wristy thing – distrust.

Trust, if you ask me, which of course
you do not, is simpleton magic, yacky,
for the ongoing is link in the chain,
I lean over to understand your clothes.

I lean over. Full stop. And that's sweet.
I have been many beens where you
have never been, sweet pigeons, ah,
I have walked even the places where

I refused to walk. All forward pleases;
please walk there and come back for me,
if I need that. Oh, calm down, senator,
it is just the changing. Pull your socks.

One girl learns her fourth chord and life
gets more calculable. I will tumble, fine
but quicken your teeth, see straightest.
You have to best me see, you have to.

## Rock Chicks / Double Decker

*It's the quiet ones.* Those who mingle at the brink
of the moshpit, ready for a barge. Badged up
because they were girl guides once and can sew.
Soft-haired boys didn't work them; the chasm,
the occult is what knocks their tummies, and red,
black and the unlamped sepulchre of their skulls.
Holsters and mayhem, an air punch. JD. Pretence.
But best pretence. To witch you need calm, to calm
you need witch. Here is their bedroom, and its door
primed with a sign, Do Not Enter Within. And don't.
I unwrap the chocolate, unpleasantly biscuity, feel
like a dolphin eating a mangetout or a prize ram
dipping into a tub of ribs. This is not me. And yet
I would paint you if I could, our Mona Lisa, which
Renaissance artist would not, Claire, solved one,
sorter, talker? The girls at this rock bar are denimy;
they ask how I know you and chocolate smidgens
are falling below me. They bam up the jukebox:
it's 'Kashmir' then 'Leather and Lace'. It's late.
I'm out of place. Rock swerved from the blues,
it did, and some form of light came, with blisters.
In the backroom venue, there are horned hands
and headbangs; simple fun is claiming its own.
As if. For all walk all roads, all eat both levels,
both candy and the candleless. Then we float
to the street end where we stand, unpainted,
unsugared, second marking our reckonings
of the rose-like replications we still might be.

## So Much Synth (Mix Tape, Slight Return)

If it is 1983, I am too shy to know America
beyond the yellow map block. Nor do I consider
you may be there, awkward, clutching a flame of words
I don't yet see. Is it California? Is there *Thriller*,

*ET*, one road which ends at Chicago, 'place of onions'.
When I combed my fringe, it reached to my chin,
Oakey, Kerr, Bob Smith. I know the score here, Brenda.
I was the 80s. Grensons, Marlboro, pretty boy, Corbijn

would have photoed me. I combed the *NME* for synth
hip, synth guts. There were boys in enclaves stabbing
their Casios, Rimmel-lipped. I knew that Hooky
could have Sylvian in a fist fight, I couldn't play

or fight, and girls were just boys without stabilisers.
I joined the army of myself, John Peel mulling on tranny;
a friend I forgot to meet. I still had a paper round
and not-the-first of the alt lives I have lived, lived.

(Recently I have been making movies but once I shifted synth
in bundles. Your mix tape? I was and am on it, ever envious,
eyeing the front man's perch, where he swings on the mic,
his bad moustached wingman pushing the white keys.

I never did win, always banging twopennies into
the synth bandit and coming up 'bell, bell, cherry',
which was the name of my first EP, three lightning strikes
of shebang. And there you were, 13, mainlining

A Flock of Seagulls. Sunglasses and disregard your triplets.)
I owe you, girl, and always will, heroine, a lap ahead.
But then you were 13. And I had serious, consuming hair
and was in a band. Our synth player is now head

of maths at my old school. No dream, Brenda, is worth
falling asleep for, unless you can wake screaming,
hands at your own throat, knowing, soundtracked and shaking
that synth was not chintz but our own breath. That's the truth.

You learn the head bob thing. All synth requires is that
and a downturned mouth. Now we are driving cross country.
Change the tape. Pass me a brownie. Track 3, Side 2.
Yes, that's the one. You get all this I guess. For you, only you.

## ‘Tender Object’ / Cats on Windowsill

Eight swans on the Princess pond, four each for these
two powsers on an LA sill, breeze-scuffed, eyes

sun-keen, on, reflectionless. Hubbub of the arcade
nonplusses, nonplus being default. Nothing said

springs roses for them or malaises, this backwater
street has known so many baskers, napped floaters

of the feline clique, soft on each other, but with claw
ever primed. Numb to the newscast, numb to the law

of losing face. Here on the mean time line, weeks,
it feels, away from LA kits, there’s icy grim, chic

cold misery, but nothing unkind beyond the pane,
no buzzsaws, no rasp or threnodic mewing. The main

deal is that we all are on. Swans on pond. Powsers
on sill and quiet is our only shroud. Winners, losers.

## KIPPERS AND GLITTER

Teddy bear maker!!!!! I want it! X

ISABELLE BOYER

## The Hoopoe

Park Güell, Barcelona and it is bench
and crossword, cryptic, and so I coach

PoB on the odd rules of the puzzle. How to
solve the Ximenean code, dive into

the mystic of one down and one across.
We walk towards ice cream and there it is:

a hoopoe on a branch. 'A hoopee?' she says.
Hoopee. I go sweet for this still on anxious days.

The ice cream is blackcurrant and we move
towards a bar, in heat. Uneven love

is the toughest of all our clues, all aching
and yet one night a month on, she wakes me:

'I liked the hoopee,' talking in her sleep.
Which is all the answer I will ever need.

## Bella # 16

When these days come when I miss you this much,
steam rises off me, steam from all of garish history
and steam from my most simple and best of thoughts.

People count on fingers to stave the lack of fortune;
light fails, but light I see by, soldiering, desperate
to be a man of sorts. Rain continues, or falters so.

Here, I have a book of signatures, not real I admit,
of those whose paths I passed in a wood at night.
When did I last light a good fire and did it warm you?

I am hanging on the dumbdown of all absolute
and you know where I am and we think that itchy.
I am not itchy, I am all candyfloss and am drifty.

But I am certain, or near to certain I am certain.
I know my capital. Low roads lead mainly south.
Minor highways ignore our subtle heartbursts.

You sleep and I must continue with the progress
towards your bidden sleep. Unwelcome, Magellan
seeing to an island he knew was not to be landed.

What do I miss? Oh, you and any blessed thing
that has to be watched till it horizons. Blunt zero
will not do me. I need the hammers and the tacks.

I am after and ever after. I bow and give in on that.
There is a reach to missing. Someone is walking
at that wood's edge and in paleness does not see me.

South. Is that it? Drift? No, I miss you and that's it.
I can sit here counting my things, but it will never be
the signed deal. The hand-in-hand walk thereafter.

## Bella #19

To dip a strange toe into another's strangeness.
To not wish a square jaw or a summer dress.

We'll go with our fear of voice, or more
the voices of our fears. That swing door

betrays our future. Behind it, one we will thank
for love or kindness; the evening's drink

is settling. We need not bear the other's staidness.
Better the wayward sideways of kindness

that are not us. To love wrong is to love still.
Who doesn't want the night? It's slippy sill

of possibilities. I need the fright of it; half
of all I am is suremost sum of all I am of.

So when I say 'I love you' and your answer comes
ten seconds later, 'thank you', raise the times

I just could not and needed other fire. We dare
both passions and impassions. Think then. Here

a spilling back. We did not and we never knew.
And sure, I would prefer, 'I love you too.'

I know what I don't want and here it is:
this mercy, that unquiet, all enchantedness.

## The Perfect Kiss

My giglet, my best-voiced sorrow, my magnum opus,
my mappa mundi, my paragon, my casino, my filet
mignon, my bichon frise, my Bang and Olufsen,
my kaleidoscope, my all-clear, my soma, my duvet,

my exquisite source, my Sunday best, my sirena,
my soonest sunrise, my alibi, my vintage port,
my cloth-shone brogue, my naked tease, my safety net,
my plum, my plume of feathers, my feather bed,

my candyfloss, my gyroscope, my perfect circle,
my new trapeze, my port and starboard, my then,
my strolling zenith, my marvel hug, my tidal wave,
my port in a storm, a storm you one night sent my way,

my gift wrap, my capital city, my communion morn,
my oil lamp, my ormolu, my perfect kiss, my howdy,
my tender star, my ribbon girl, my last hello, my selection,
my monolith, my eureka day, my farewell song sung long.

## Musette / Cilice

This hour of the supermoon night, I play
my musette and all the neighbours ache
at the chanters' double burst. I'd cease,
but these spikes around my thigh mean
I need for treacle, the canticles I whittle
from this bag of velvet with squid arms.

I know where cherries hang, what boxes
hold. How to damn any man. To charm
is plus though. And here is that music.
Pain prompts so I tighten my device.
Gain arrives. Fieldfares and stonechats
quiver from sleepy nests. Best of gold

sits deep and we pipers force its rise.
But strip these bothers off me;
I did not mean to swerve this way,
the wrong way round the board
though I will play again tomorrow;
pain plus melody our clearest pleasure.

## Simple Dish / Speedboat

Nothing fennel, nothing pawpaw, just a sauce
you'd ride to, decent. Chicken, yes, and chilli,
for a little fire to heat the head. Some little salt,
some stock, but let that be now. Simple dish.
The infant lies thumbsucking, and seems tattooed,
though it is not that, since his father spent
this warm afternoon painting out this scene
on his wriggling back: a speedboat that splits
the Volga. It's blue on blue. The child lies there,
happy enough, as his life will be, portraying.

# Caramac / Grand Romance

Living four flights up means you have to decide
between Caramac and romance, two ecosystems
I am avoiding. When I think I find what is wrong
with Caramac, I find I think what is wrong with me.
Someone tonight said romance is dead and now
I am sneaking on its corpse, with the stolen key
to the mortuary snucked into my jeans. Silence.
And I approach romance and kiss its tagged toe.
I knew it. It was a giddy darling, also a blaggard.
I knew it. The spring streams, supervoice, clear.
My arms out, blissing. The dark or the sweet sweet,
the pull-up. You can romance the dark, I presume,
or Caramac the dark, or talk however way too much
about the dark. Or girls you met on corners, shy.
Where romance lurks or imitates the hoverfly
there is a brook which will insist in its rolling.
The plague year people had their romance, it threw
them high while they crumbled. I've been gnat close
to ardour and flinched. You know, crystal appears,
linen drapes you, sugar dissolves without heat.
You walk home like cherryade pouring into
a Cupid's bow mouth. You start to tell the truth,
for hours even. The business is that the business
of the best of things is to be avoided. For we go
to that ultimate from which we can only return,
dropping, gasping hearted. Shall we risk it again?
Do we walk in the direction where whichever dare
might chomp us? Oh, I see us all zombieing, all
torn towards the code we think we have solved.
Rolls Royce Caramac. Right honourable Caramac.
We kid ourselves by the hiding of it from ourselves.
But it's there below the cactus, or in a bedside drawer.
I knew I must reach for it. We now must split the bar.

## Hate

a thing with mirrors;
the rough trampoline of romance;
turquoise rubbed through a sieve;
the wrong route to the wrong thing.

Don't knock it; like the ichneumon wasp
it has its job, half of our heart,
a caustic beauty with one cruel limb,
its bra strap drooping on the arm of all need.

Some day, in Truro or Oslo, you'll need me
and will cramp my memory to you,
knowing that we were, that your most moment
was when you reddened, shivered and felt it.

## Work Crush

It is just past two and suddenly, little Paul
from Accounts steals your eye, his shirt
is somehow stirring, not what he was before.
Or Deborah, her sweater blooming, bites
her bottom lip and all the hormones trip.
Oh no, it's teacher with his manner, nurse
with her supposed sorting, the fireman
holding out the form to confirm that he
has extinguished, though he hasn't, your fire.
Daft guff. We zombie into this marzipan
of possibility. Fergus, I am repeating
your name on the train. Marie, I saw you
opening your Tupperware and ripened.
We are singletons but we could jet off
to somewhere darling, our cases twinned
in pastel shades. Our lives would lift
into that starling swarm of whatever.
I barely know you and yet you may
be welcome at my funeral, karaokeing
my best song. The giddy spreadsheet
is in downfall. I have nothing, nothing
this evening but telly and ready meal.
My friends swell to a crushing chorus,
though none of them singing anywhere
other than my tragic within. Large glass
of wine, anyone? I have itches and stuff
to go through: photocopier bullfight,
clockwatch, the dumb arousal of us,
who ought to know better. Shall we?
Or to travel alone. I scheme myself
into your spooning, dream of breakfast,
togetherness, warm oil, simple talk
that only the easy ones have, the doomed,
the happy few who are going, kissing,
towards a zone the many will never rule.

## Baby's Cute and Mummy Too

The Finns don't have a dream,
they *see* one.
The Zulus *meet* a dream as if it were
a halfway thing.
Whether a good or a bad, Azeris
*suffer* a dream.

And as I see it, the life and the dreamt
are as to a charm-heavy child
and her flawless mother.
One cross-legged, devout above
her coloured blocks and populace of dolls,
the other standing at the hallway table,
chancing the day in blue.
But flawless? There is no such thing.

And yet, we dream of it
and wake half smiling.
Those who reached the core and pips
of the maze threw high their hands
and roared, forgetting that
the way out is much tougher
and that night approached.

# False Flags / Khaki

In 1848, Lieutenant-General Sir Harry Burnett 'Joe' Lumsden originated the khaki uniform that later became standard for the British Army.

'I saw some crazy dream,' says the Finnish Dancer
who an hour ago has been skimmed to sleeping
on the leather couch a puckle of feet behind me,
listening to Massive. 'False Flags' is what plays
and I think of what my family gave this world:
khaki. How odd, though life is a mix of nuts,
that my great-great whatever, the commandant,
would shift the shade of uniform, switching it.
What grandfather would pull on at the Somme,
my father in Egypt. Soil, drab. Pale end of beige.
Us Lumsdens sometimes err and beige things up.
Or don't err, and we save you. Take your chance.
Pause. Ever met my eye? Did I redress, address
or, pity sakes, undress you? Oh, I only meant
to khaki you. To send you to the billet suave
and to some battle sweet. Natty, unseeable
in not the colour that. Throw off your redcap,
your jerkin of lavender. These are now our rules.
Set sail for Abyssinia and the veldt. Best boy,
Lumsden of the Guides has dressed you right.
I whisper camouflage, for this is night, and all
might rage. The bullet take you, love ignite you.
Oh, did I say love? I am conflating. False flags
sail under the colours of a one or another
who yanked my heart. I fear my violin is out
and I am playing 'Hearts and Flowers'. Joe,
you saw out mutiny, by the age's necessity
not in 'deep politics' or 'the constant present'.
You brought off dying, which I have not earned.
Still standing down myself. In what I choose
to wear, so rarely pretty, and rarely khaki.

But dreams come, fears, and silky understandings,
simple situations we'd face to face about.
The Dancer wakes and seals the other couch.
I hanker vicious colours but am waning.
Unlikely to die tonight. None unexpected.
And pause. I matter but I will not matter.

## Elba

When I was cast out there, I thought
of children who dance, their dibbling feet
and of feathers, how they swiff the air.
And though there were those beaches
I daydreamed of the beach, the idea as ever
higher in the chain than the actual.
I beckoned to me the words for canyon
and continent, that I could walk ten miles
not in a circle. Desert thoughts wiled me.
The sea being simple sea, and not enough.
In my games all cards were trumps, I lost
and won each game. Treason was impossible.
What won me was simplicity, the sweeping,
the bedmaking, the birdless birdcage gaping.
To sneeze was fetish, to sprint was fetish,
though I was near to done with sprinting.
Talking to myself I kept to afternoons,
ambition was a concept I cleaned clear
off my plate, which was blue and one-off.
So I have no favourite colour. All enemies
have me down wrong. I have duchesses
who dreamed me, gilded and musky ladies.
I am lying and all art supposes to the lie.
All. If I squint I can see the edge of Tuscany
and the truth. This late night, this sad art,
this urge. Commander, you kinked the world.
I kink my little system, which barely ticks.
I have nothing roasting and no one phoning;
the trick is to know what you will never be
and the where. The Elba. Yet all us damned
exile ourselves, sail sweet towards the island.

## My Kleos

A gracious death will add seven to it. I sit,
hands knitted at my nape, sure champion.
Top trump. And legs up, lest my boldened feet
niggle the earth and take root as stout aspen.

I bat off foisting kittens, the glory seeking
vulgus, badly wrapped and wrongly cued.
My hugeness and this slick, ironic bleating
which saps your simple pity, piques your feud,

they fill the room, though better call it chamber,
for no God took a lift or drove a dodgem.
My chiselled chassis's marble; heart of amber.
I flood the centrefold, I tamp the chasm.

Rock of Ages. Anchor. Answers on a card.
To which I will not guarantee reply.
I toil, though sweatless, minting the true word.
You sense my grace, horripilate nearby.

## May ’15 EP

*Through Vicarage Avenue*

Rain knocks the pollen from its packets
and my eyes doggy paddle. Ne’er-do-well daisies
pitch through turf, inch-high questers.

Friday, and which of many boons shall I invoke?
To watch this woman in front of me, slender
of neck, her back tattooed with Mercator’s folly.

Wrong world. But I am Standard now, not Village.
I swim to the wrong world, past the icky church
where squealers go to ease their jerky ills.

Slow spree of teatime. My average height,
my average weight squat awkward on the day,
pitched between the rose and violet truffle

of content and the psoriasis of all quotidian. Through.
Wrong. Pitch. Brand names of self-bloom. Grey Day.
The Standard’s lights are dimmed. No one I know.

## *Cameron*

Not a metaphor and let's not cheapen this
by saying *memory*. Not that, but a reservoir
where once we let a hedgehog go, belting
into the ferns. I had a Scottish education.

Back when that meant. Here is my grammar,
my topological purity. My 'test your strength'
machine flashing in your bonce's fairground.
The hammer yours to grab, pinhead, sparrow.

Cameron: flat, bonnie and bosky, mid-Kingdom.
Barely a village. Reservoir surface at equal
depth from near sight to farthest. A jerkin
pulled round my stocky boyhood; sandshoes.

I do not doubt the present. Infectious, yes,
in all its senses. Here is my frown, beneath
my crown of authority. I am indeed someone.
But let go. Pin-eyed, through these ferns.

Yet someone is in charge of me. Oh hell.
*Shall we go for a run in the car*, says Dad.
It was barely a village and now I look it up.
It does not exist. I type my name, but pause.

The vatic thermometer drops. I may not either.

## *At The Standard*

*I cried all morning*, said Francesca.
*It's bad*, I said. *It's bad*, came her echo
Wrong world. *A pint of Becks please*,
this to the barmaid, *and a cure for hay fever.*
*Get pregnant*, she says. It works. Wrong
crawls all over the menu here. Spoilt
when our wallet spills. Once, we had
powsowdie, then microwaved macaroni.
Now our buns are glazed, omega seeds
are scattered. *Make the profiteroles large*
*to share*. That polecat rubs his mitts
in number ten. There is summer slaw,
kale pesto. Everything comes smothered.
Skin-on. Quinoa rules this establishment.
Standard. Sourdough, stout-cured, heritage.
I picture Cameron, ginger ale ketchup
infecting the razored gant where his chin
might have developed. *I've heard of it*,
is the most he can offer on disbelief.
Deep in the caliphate, knives are whetted.
America boils on borrowed gas. Baby gem
sounds tasty, but I long back sussed
that life is largely lies swanked up
and fed to you cold. Dearie me, fuck this.

## Hoverfly

* lovely cloud-headed girl of the bee-wasp nexus * steadfast standout of the graveyard's sunflood * face which blissed up in the psychomanteum's witching hour * deemed unsinister, an itch on the wrist of hindsight *

## Halfway Through the Year of the Goat

The walk from premise to promise. Ten of us
homeward from the bonspiel, one icy midnight.
And not a song, just whispers, which are music
of a sort. Or seven of us, young and marching

from Strath to town, on a night without lights.
Or the backroads of Jersey, where we barely
saw each other, back to the converted church.
Starlit peregrinations, mirky walks to our beds.

Long coats, headlong impetus, the party over
and the awkward comfort of the trudge. Now,
and now again, the late bleat of a nanny goat
nosing the barbed wire. Will someone love us?

Will bed accept us? Far seems now a significant
species of far. Tempted now to tell our stories,
tail up or tail down, but stories fall in the chase
of all honesty versus songwork versus silence.

Each of us will dream of the goat, her milling,
her lonesome blur, her noise of a poorly child.
We have all been somewhere, and the elastic
of home sense is pulling. Yet we do not sing,

though we want to, we want to, halfway now,
sorry in our wind-down, knowing the promise
gone. Some could break into song, the rest of us
rest, song lacing our blood. That is how we sleep.

## Twenty-four Hours of People Saying Nope

Nope says Charles, in Topeka, Kansas,
I do not need that much gas. Nope says
Jillian, I do not need to keep this book.
Nope declares Faycal, everyone talks
to themselves and they are lying if they
say they don't. Nope says Calum, quietly,
the shop will not be open at this hour.
Nope says the ghost of Ted Berrigan,
I am tempted but have no plans today
to return to you. Nope says a tall man,
whose name we do not know, in Osler,
Saskatchewan, I am not ready for another.
Nope says Daisy, and that is all she says.
Nope says Alice, in Perth, Australia,
I do not need more pasta, the cupboard
is busting with it. Nope, says Melvin,
I will not change this song. Nope says
Kelly, I am young but sledging is not
as perilous as you suggest. Nope says
Anthony, his scalp shining, I will do
what I have to, and abseiling is involved.
Nope is heard in the lavatory cubicle
next to yours and you know by now
you will never know why. Nope echoes
in an alley you are walking on and it is
Amanda and Larry and you can hunch
what she is saying nope to. Nope drifts
on the park, its bad mouth uncredited.
Nope says Louise, in Dublin, a mist
crawling on, I don't have the patience.
Nope says Marie, you will have to lift me.
Nope whispered, an ouchy knockback.
Patti Smith noping, she has overherbed
a casserole. Oh lordy, nope is climbing

on our soft backs. Nope, says Joshua,
I've been through this too many times,
in a suburb of Aberdeen. Nope,
overheard at a rainy station, the bus
replacement service won't do.
Nope says Malcolm, I already have
several of those. Nope says Marjorie,
glancing from her buggy, I will not
be changing my mind. Nope is ruling
our ability to nope. Nope says Carmel,
Bailey's on her chin, I will never agree
with your ideas on the semantic. Nope
I say disappearing into necessary hush.

## Time Loop / Wishing Wells

Then you put the ball into the air.
It is table tennis or maybe it is pinball
and the ball skids down. You did it
on the last go; the bastard ball returns.
You punt or lob or wellie but the ball
returns to blessed earth. So I did this
ten minutes back and here I am shaping
the make of a man lifting a ball into air.
Again. Spit out gravity, since it is time
which needs us to count on its fingers.
Ten minutes ago, I wrote these words.
Ten minutes; now I think I think them.
They knew me first, I fear, another me
went first and thought them. Don't like
the other me, he has gained weight
and he likes Spiderman movies. Now,
it is ten minutes later and I am me again.
Bristly, sipping. Ah, do you remember
when we met up ten minutes past?
I liked what you will say in ten minutes.
Loop. Let's meet yesterday of sorts.
I'll find where you were. At Waterloo.
Or by the wishing well, throwing down
a fivepenny. Your wish is for worldness,
or a BMX, or to sleep tonight. The coin
takes ten minutes to drop, then you find
it is there in your hand again, the wish
quavering, without patience, the young,
juicy brain which gets all I don't, wagging,
the tail of a dog I saw ten minutes back
and expect to meet around this corner.
Hello, puppy, I wished for you or did
ten minutes back or will in ten. Hello,
let me scruff your scurfy back. We may
need each other where we are heading next.

## Small Calamities

A little litter – a fankle of lesser purposelessness
on a dipping wynd. A comfy chair which wasn't.
When the protective edges towards awkward.
An empty bottle you somehow can't throw
either into the skip or the sea. Grass yellowing.
Are you with me? I fear you all are not. Stains,
limited gain, a switch you switch and switch.
An itch. A pot plant failing to dare to flower.
Fur wrong napped: you stroked the cat from back
to front. The orchestra seem tense. Some texter
walks at you. The shiver at the end of any season.
The wrong song at the end of anything. Dreams
which did not build. Sense which makes sense
and so irks. I have been these. I have dealt out
these waxy cards. Envelopes which try our trust.
Rubble is a dry word which turns me nervy.
Can't say quite right why. Eyes of hungry dogs.
Mirrors, all mirrors, and all songs about them.
Tickets and their purpose. That some worthy
might ask something of me. I am pretender.
Hangnail. Paper cut. A sorry task you walk to
with head downsome. Risk. The heart thunders
when a cab does not arrive. All the countries
which you will not visit. The concept of visit.
All we must recover from. Seedy minor dramas.
A hole in something. Rust. A dish overcooked.
Am I flapping? Reaching Jersey, when we thought
we would do Bologna. Aching to kiss a throat.
Windscreen wipers of interior dilemma. Angst
of shadow shift. I am spreading all of this now
on the tablecloth of collective apprehension.
A possible smell of burning. Friends, tomorrow
will be better. Every cursed thing will walk kind.
Honeys, everything will be kippers and glitter.

## Jean Tester / Lionesses

Here is my story of how things are written,
spoken and given. Best to listen to me now.
It is 1383 and a brewer is setting to his task
of making brew. Lion beer. Ja, Löwenbräu.
Courage is part liquid, part pretending. Hold
to task, testa, seed coat, shield. Protect,
and hold the boy, small one to the smaller.
Motherdom is seemly work. Pride is what?
The solemn boys, the ready girls, eager
to provide, destroy. The restless gazelles
huddle and seek the drinking pool, eyes
ever sifting for danger, keystone predators.
You have your pint, but a cheeky chaser
would help to get you there, sleepy, there
on the savannah of the end of some night.
Whatever gets you through one where grief
is kicking like a catty glyph in a bestiary.
Lionesses, I forgive you. Some sad days
beg for comfort. Motherhug. Downtime.
Jean, I never knew you but your boy is fine.
The lioness is a pussycat in her shell
of fuzz. All mothers lie the night in fuss
of plausible wrong. Protection takes hold
of blood. The lioness sings her nocturne.
In Charlton or in Transvaal, same deal.
Here is my story of how things are written,
spoken and given. By which I mean solution.
The lioness blinks and she nudges her cub.
The brewer makes his brew since our need
is what need does. The mother spins love.
Best mothers do. Bravo. Best mothers are.

## Tending to the Reliable

And all sneezing darkly in the dimming divide.
JOANNA NEWSOM, 'Peach, Plum, Pear'

You get what I like. That field of daffodils.
The wonderful girl on the bicycle. Toffee,
if well provided. I shall not list, I am not
some biblical prophet. But hey, you lean,
you need to. You keep things dry and safe,
for the sparest days. Friendship, medicine.
Roller skates, a dippy mystery. You tend,
your bosom moving needfully, you regard
regard itself. The cans of soup you may well
never open. A friend you feel you can call.
Discipline, I am conjoining, baddest buddy
but reliable. Clocks, I'm cynical but need you.
Fallback, harness. The sylphy skewer you dig
into a chicken mostly roasted. I do promise
to stop this listing. People have torpid things
they need to assess, gaps in their emotional
undercurrent. You know your one to twelve
in several major languages but you diff off
in the teens. And it would hurt to be caught.
I need a duvet on me. I need the timidity
of some, the vividity of others. This late,
I seek the links I followed and I boosted.
Routes, boltholes. A calm I dwindle over
then recalibrate. This system-diving beyonds
the divide. Rotations begin, chemicals rut,
the unhuman peeks from behind that screen.
Scratch at it and it might take you, sneeze
and you're floored: now someone in an alley,
halfway along, alone, in a sour flood of angst.
Count your books. See where need sends.
What is in these wardrobes? The elegant

yawn and somewhat Braille of what I kept.
To rely on. I will suffer long friendships.
I will lean to the weather. I do want days
which flush from bright to grey. Lovers
who settle to an alternative importance. But
I need to be lost at this airport, my passport
in a bedside drawer and to rely on possibility,
that bastard way in, that bastard way out.

## Ashna Sarkar, Aged 5

on her first bike. To rule the universe
is not enough. To mow down some pigeons
then rule the show might do. To be Rameses
would work. Rameses, Evita and Genghis
and Jehanne d'Arc and perhaps St Columba too.
Determined. Get off her pavement. Learn
the rules. Who rules. The helmet's a ruse.
She'd never fall. The battling star of this.
The all. Sandals carambaing. Power ranger,
pedalling. A small big bang. A cosmic blur.
She's halfway up Ermine Street. The burn
of all future is on her and she ring rings
the bell, drops one paw from the handlebar,
salutes and sings the national anthem of herself.

## Halfway Through the Year of the Monkey

In these last 100 days when I
am your denizen,
silver night, great green pan
of vaganza,
music bubbles from cracks,
insists,
a prime monkey
inflating a birthday balloon and I
swear off some stuff:
metaphor, screwy girls, gumption
on others' behalf
and stick on unknown pleasures:
morphine, my ghost
unreleased, this nimbus-pawed spaniel
dozed to submission.
Music, Roddy, music. This loosening night
is nothing to it.
Vanity rules its spine. A glockenspiel
you strain now to hear, monkey rumba
played on pre-philosophy bones;
rack, rickle, spill. They open
graves these days
and do not find my worth. No animal
waltzed me well.
I wish the monkey luck, and if our genes
had failed to fade,
I'd hold her now, dear chirping thing.
Now here's my father
playing his full kit, songs for people,
snare, bass, hi-hat.
The sign outside the town (quite near
where I was attacked
by a swan during al fresco sex)
reads, it seems,

‘Welcome to St Andrews, Home of Golf.
No Monkeys. No music
without licence.’ Go figure me now.

# The End of Fanny

> I am not quite sure Regan understands that Fanny is a name (or more to the point what she thinks it is). Reading Enid Blyton's *Willow Farm* to her the other night. Fanny the cook was out collecting eggs. Regan laughing uncontrollably and said, 'Gran, you said a bad word.' I composed myself quite quickly and changed Fanny's name. Regan says, 'What happened to Fanny, Gran?' Me, 'She died.' The end.
>
> TRICIA MORRIS

Some afternoons, your name creeps up on you
and kills you young. The seventh egg drops out
of the clutching hand and you have gone to meet.

You had an omelette in mind: scallions, sage,
nothing fancy, a brisk stir and swirl and froth.
A little milk, a swish of pepper. Life simple,

until it knows you for your name and death
taps you on the apron. The breeze was swift
that day but you thought surest to outlive it.

You, Fanny, who never did exist, then age
grasped you and you existed less. Your youth
being no excuse. Twitchy pigeons in the loft

rouse Willow Farm; the kitchen help lies dead.
Pigs wrestle in the sty. Tractors plough land.
And now we call you Hannah, Pam or Rachel.

The tale moves on, though you lie quiet, soft
in soil. All names are danger. We did not choose
our names, damned by or stuck with them. The end.

MIX
Paper from
responsible sources
FSC® C007785
FSC
www.fsc.org